THISTLE

Thistle

poems

Melissa Kwasny

LOST HORSE PRESS
SANDPOINT · IDAHO

ACKNOWLEDGMENTS

Grateful acknowledgment is made to the editors of the journals in which the following poems first appeared:

Amherst Review: "Aspen" and "Mountain Holly"
Bellingham Review: "Tobacco"
Crab Orchard Review: "Jasmine"
Cutbank: "Chokecherries"
Feminist Studies: "Fern" and "Iris"
Fine Madness: "Nightshade" and "Water Birch"
Many Mountains Moving: "Salsify"
Nimrod: "Rose Hip," "Laurel," "Willow," "Balsam," "Hawthorn," and "Rue"
Poetry Northwest: "White Clover," "Juniper," "Tree Lichen," and "Icelandic Poppies"
Puerto del Sol: "Mullein" and "Violets"
Rhino: "Prairie Sage" and "Moss"
South Dakota Review: "Kinnikinnick," "Cattails," and "Thistle"
Three Penny Review: "Berries"

I would also like to thank Patricia Goedicke, Robert Baker, Rusty Morrison, Sheila Black, Martha Sutro, Grace Grafton, and Greg Pape for their careful reading of these poems.

The italicized lines in "Thistle" are from Ezra Pound's "The River Merchant's Wife: A Letter" and in "Icelandic Poppies" from John Keats' "Ode to Autumn."

Book Design by Christine Holbert

FIRST EDITION

LIBRARY OF CONGRESS CATALOGUING IN PUBLICATION DATA

Kwasny, Melissa, 1954–
  Thistle: poems / by Melissa Kwasny.
      p. cm.
  ISBN-13: 978-0-9762114-1-9 (alk. paper)
  I. Title.
PS3561.W447T47 2006
811'.54—dc22

                              2005037294

CONTENTS

The career of flowers differs from ours
only in audibleness.

—*from the letters of Emily Dickinson*

I

RUE

Who will accompany me to the roots
of this sadness
which dangle like cutworms, angel hair?

Men won't get close to it. Something
too heavy-handed.
The lids. The stoop. The clothes too large.

But the women are tender. They recognize
my face, a moon
that erases itself as it travels. They feed me

rice, light as moth wings, the yellowed toes
of garlic. They send me
home with hummus and cuttings of rue.

I remark on its prettiness, but I don't know
what to do with it.
Witch's herb, they say, antidote for poison.

So, what do they think? That my father
molested me? That my mother
thrust an unbent hanger into her womb?

Who knows about those years when
anything could happen?
The milk spills in the grass, open to infection.

Carry something light, they say, a leaf
like a child's mitt, the shape
Matisse cut out when he was too old to paint.

Handmaiden. Sister to the vetch. Should I
tuck it behind my ear,
its string of lakes, the estuary of its stem?

Should I carry it with me down the slick
black steps of memory
at night when water rises, slow as in a dirge?

Tiny, smug. But what if there isn't any poison,
if I can't see
what has happened? What if it's my fault?

BLUEBELL

In seeps near the mud-hatch,
the dark wet suits
of alder, insect legs
stapled around each blade.

Everything warns against approach,
thistle, the shadow,
moss-pelt on the step-stones.

Slump-shouldered and ragged
in a sway of benediction,
the bluebells
I can just make out in the shade.

They are pebbles meant to fall,
these petals
death-bent, imperfect.
Are all plants this *effeminate*?

Like butterflies, the leaves
cling to the stalk
to dry their rain-pinched wings.

If you have bells, then ring, heart
of the overcast,
bog-god of the bitter.
I will learn to kneel to hear you.

YARROW

Filament. Less than a footstep.
What are you
next to the cave,
the barrel-chest of the heart?

No one trusts
anything but the largest shadows.
Not froth. Nerve flower.
The inconsistency of my intent.

If I take the fragrant, open pouch
of your hand, who will know me
without my wound?
How will I recognize myself?

Though I want to be like you, fresh,
a swathe of healing,
tender with the knowledge
that each day comes to me, astir

with heat or rain—I am mud.
Your company. Your interference.
While you are green
pillowed under the skin of apples.

Look, I didn't try to find you.
You were silver-stemmed like stars,
divaricate,
and called from the dark ground.

Not to cure sadness, but to find it,
to close the raw throat.
We are different. They
could never make you hate yourself.

OLD WORLD ROSE

Each mortal thing does one thing and the same:
Deals out that being indoors each one dwells.
—*Gerard Manley Hopkins*

I dig the bed deep, two feet by two feet
to leave, as the instructions say, root-room,
though worlds of wanwood leafmeal lie, add peat
and steer manure and place the stones, assume
that I'll forget and mow it. It's tiny now,
a dark green shred of faith, held up by earth
I pack around it. The herbals say that starting

plants respond to curse and blessing. Allow
that it was hybridized my year of birth.
Honey-bronze. Yet very winter hardy.

Our words were simple. Rose, not eglantine.
I taught myself to draw them as a child.
I remember mastering the spiral line
that began as point, then lapped and lapped like wind
unevenly in to its outside petals.
The leaves I drew were never true, not stiff,
nor was I awful like the photos said.
I dozed against them, dozed and let the nettles
pass: My face? My awful face, my life?
As if one could choose the good house or the bad.

What kind of perfume does so and so wear,
she said, I don't think you have enough time for me.
Here means the house, the work involved. Here
where we do the wash. We don't say laundry.
July and the green world is turning blue,
the world that is divided into poor
and rich. It is always *them* who are unhappy.
I need: you, a god, pliancy. May the muse
wet my lips. And sometimes she is sore
and comes not. To need something rose so badly.

To cleave in all its forms. Cleft,
cloven. Toe-flowers,
the raffle of soft white thorns.

If there are involuntary muscles
in the claws of these birds
to keep them perched while they

sleep, what is involuntary in me?
Breath, the heart,
maybe this impulse to do nothing

but watch. How hard can it be
to enjoy your life,
to lie down in the mussed green

bed of the senses, this rag garden,
the triumvirate leaves.
In clover. You can't just live here

like a swarm of faint-hearted bees,
clogged with emotion.
But really, what is there to do?

Lost days of summer when I produce
nothing but self-complaint:
To be pure is to believe in the search

for your own goodness, pulling each
petal like meat from
between the teeth. Will it be sweet?

MULLEIN

Soft as the deaf, as tightly
budded, even my name hides
under the tongue,
burrows into me like an infection.

Mallow. Cob. I am host
with a hundred ears. What is here
feeds, golden and small,
unable to fly away from me.

Still here in the stair-step fall
of light, I am infiltrated
with aphids and ants
that stick to the glue of my veins.

No one accepts what life offers.
Too common to thrive
by the roadside, soft as the roadside
dust that covers me, and thus,

get the poison meant for others—
the noxious, the invasive,
meaning your fear of cancer.
To thrive, you say, is monstrous.

Who can blame me that I prefer
poor soil, that I ask
for rolled oats without milk
in this land in love with plenty?

How long can you stay angry?
I rise out of the green
and obscure, a flamboyant stalk,
muscled, a landmark in the field.

Look around you. You will see
the brown shells of my last resistance.
Immune to what?
I am soft as exhaustion, soft as ash.

NETTLES

Voices from the path through nettles
Come to us on your hands
Alone with your lamp
Only your hand to read
—*Paul Celan*

Against me: all of it, the ash in my soup,
the straw-like hem of my sleeves.
The busy satellites, like mice hunting grain,
keep changing direction.

August, and I try to sleep under stars
that starch and thicken
while the day-air shakes out its wings.
I can hardly wait to tell you: I hate! I hate!

The Icelandic poppies don't last in this heat.
Their scarlet fades by afternoon.
And the polar icecaps—those immortal truths—
dribble through Canada but don't reach here.

Helicopters bleat as they hover over the pond,
scoop up a basket for the forest thirst.
Oh, summer, my body is open-mouthed like a fish.
The hours on the bird clock sound shrill.

Lash my arthritic hands. The fire will take
my mistakes. The stones,
the stones will correct them. I only
dream that my hands are bitten by small dogs.

Nettle is the green beak that nips, and guards
the eerie swing of the low stream.
Nettle is the hard path, the one I should abide by.
Arrogance, that sting. My life is pocked with it.

At last, we come to you after a summer
of the delicate:
arugula, cilantro, the bib-leafed lettuces.

Folded over the withered peas, carrots
raw-scalped from frost,
the belts of your contortions remain green.

You were the first thin plumes of spring,
so much of what
was to be expected, straight shot to the sun.

But then came your maturity, so odd
we were afraid to touch you,
when you grew the sperm-shaped, the six-

bulbed stars and exposed those bulbs to air.
To say you flaunted them
is not too extreme. You, the family curiosity.

You wear the tail-feathers of a poppycock,
party hat of a Venetian,
with green, pink and wood-pale streamers.

Lost, we say, in the gyrations that walked
you here from sands
and slaves, your petals their favorite meat.

Admit it. You revel in your mutancy.
You stretch, fail,
and drop, weighted by your eccentricities,

ancient as Egypt, yet harmless.
Then why does it still shock us, perversity
that masquerades for your resurrection?

FIREWEED

Junction. The mud is black-jowled.
Wild geranium, the wick

of fireweed gone to froth.
Strewn, the evangelical spread

of alder leaf, the riparian ash,
all the yellow spades of aspen.

Horsemint, umbel of the hemlock,
poisonous. Now past their prime,

the brick-eyed and green
bottle-flies shine like car fenders.

No, it is never enough to name
what we love, the whorl

of the cup, enjambment of the current,
though they slip through the land,

tarrying at our doors to speak in tongues.
Here a constellation holds

together by the merest string and tackle.
A measure of our lust, we ask for more.

TREE LICHEN

You. What I pick from my clothes.
The last shreds of disaster.
The soap-blue splat of kingdom come.

What I have left on the line, a frayed
thread caught on the jagged nail,
the forgotten hose swollen with ice.

Spineless. You are stemmy and dry
as the teased hair of women.
Creek-side, when your chartreuse tangles.

To survive on so little, the vertical
soil of bark, and snow to suck
where it lands. You take no chances,

but lean out some to catch the light,
splayed like a cell only this
is your body, simple, a sea-blue caulk

to fill the seams, a certain height which
you have mustered.
How quickly it can all unravel, a cricket

caught by winter. Better to hunker
flat against the host,
to be so slow, outside, and still alive.

No one is looking for you, a growth
on dead limbs, stiff
and wadded like a frozen, ruffled dress.

Rootless, stemless, flowerless. What
holds you on is fear. You do
what you have always done. What is left.

THISTLE

Unrequited. That story.
Allure from the bramble. Like these petals
packed tight within the thorned
body of a flower until
their pink is compressed into fuchsia.
Royal and fly-strewn,
the thistles hang their bright heads,
a banner among the sage, the browning
grasses. Look, *the paired butterflies*
are already yellow with August.
The honey scent is grained with loam.
Thistle, then thistle,
the stalks crowd the disturbed ground.
There is an apiary atop their spindling.
Nothing I could walk through.
Nothing we could approach
without our own brand of violence.
Look at us. Each day, we grow more distant,
not touching, toward our own graves.
Is it not a lack of love, the thistle's ploy
and resistance? The flower is unguarded
when open. Yet, the leaves
and stem are fenced. Yes, I resent, and you?
You learn to live with less and less
amid the click and fizz of grasshoppers.

KINNIKINNICK

Brush it aside, the pock and hush
from its headlong dive,
snow from pine needles into snow—
Bearberries. That small red choir.

If you find them, it is only because
you have memorized
where leaves, small and shaped
like tears, spread between the granite.

Kick it back. The powdered moon.
Light no fires. In every
room, part the curtains, and if
you have a lover, notice how she ages.

Down with the crushable, where bear,
master herbalist,
claws for her fruits, the well-
wrought and plum trails of the stems.

Everything has its hole, its cave
for concealment
except timothy, blond heads
high above plumes of red and pink—

You dreamt their cry, and closer, this.
Cello. Wormwood. Low.
Who would expect green in the middle
of grief? The grandmother is dying.

Who would think to bring a sprig from
a language few speak now?
Kinnikinnick.
That which is to be mixed with the bitter.

Under the lapsed stitch of birch bark,
bronze-dark as oil,
under the inner bark I split
to steep the white pith for my tea—

look up. Our gold luck has turned
to rags. I can see the sun
on three hands now, each with
saw-toothed rays, spots from frost.

So painterly, these daubs. The limbs
so thin. A vine maybe
of earth-sparks that float, a fire
that stirs, or boils that erupt in air.

Forgive me. I have forgotten the grace
of this season, its complications,
how the earth mounds
over the suckling roots, the grass spills

so easily into beds. How my weight
is accepted among the shallows.
Pathos. Melodrama.
How I am known for my indulgences.

Wind arrives through thistle, the blush
and green rye. It is true
that it seems to come in footsteps.
And to say the hardest things so quietly.

II

ROSEMARY

Once, a dark woman fled past me
and in her haste, dropped her cloak.
It was azure. And it
has stained my pale fingers forever.

Once, the jewel I clutched to my belly
had shape. It was sharp-edged
like a star. It caught my father's words,
every coarse thread of cruelty.

Though I have lived invisible before,
a briar wood, a background
tangle of green—
If anything, I want you to remember me.

Crush me. I am susceptible
to the slightest storm, to anyone
who has the nerve to call me beautiful.

Once, I was dry as a stem, the flaming
shape of cypress. I nursed
my neglect. There was an oil to it,
too sharp to call a mother's perfume.

The milk was not hers. It was your
milk I was promised.

Children grow too large to be held
and their mothers leave them.

Here, invite me. Fragrant and bitter,
I will cling to your tongue.
Camphor. Tobacco. Sea cast with salt.

Once, I was private, exotic, disinherited
from sweetness.
Once, I held a certain beauty, stoppered.

I was planted and I was left to my own
to grow pungent, repellent.
No matter how
old you are, I am too grown up for you.

JASMINE

Bring me something rare—what seas are here
are frozen—a fume to force the bud of my heart.

My heels are scraps. All my friends' mothers
are dying. The trough is narrow and I sleep in it.

Relax. I ask for nothing dangerous—pink tips
and lacquer, the small green worm of a tongue.

Jasmine. The white-flocked hem of a secret
lifted, a confidence breached, packed into its sleek

dress, the one that darkens before it opens—a frill,
a subterfuge, the wound rain makes in the snow.

Look, I don't know what love is, or what damage
it has done to women. Our lips painted red

to resemble labia. Love as *not that*. The petals
I ask for are tender, opaque, doused in the clay

of their perfume. What they are is what I want from
you, heliotropic. Disrupt me with your lavish will.

MOUNTAIN HOLLY

Your use, your name—
How can it matter? You are small,
thorned, and dry as my heels.

The frozen water pools where
motion has bled through,
but I, like you, have retreated.

Flat against the cool, turned cheek
of earth. The drain
of volatile oils and perfume.

Did we call it on ourselves, the soft
blue drag, to wish
instead of ask? Wish instead of do?

And sleep, that marrow, the mind
shrunk back? The rusted
green thumbs show our age.

What is courage to you? Shallow
and transfixed,
I cling to the rhizome of what some

would call my life, misled, random,
even sloppy. Here,
take my hand. I want to tug you

up slowly, through the brown cloth
of your own making.

Your roots like a chain under snow.

ROSE HIP

Red pod of the rose hip, jellied from cold.
Inside, the pith-dry nest of white seeds.

It is a deflated balloon, a hood the self is
lost in. Too red, the nurse says,

having sex must be hard for you. This is not
a scab. Though it is plumped, not sweet,

it is still the first mind that spring returns to.
Green fume around the stems, the dark

pink folds that will bleach in their unraveling—
It is too early to commit to anything.

Yes, I remember the bloom, when each day
seemed contrived for my growing,

the gloss of new skies, the crowding of water.
What is hidden came to feed from my hand.

How is it I grew afraid of my pink swish
and gather, how soft my skin could become?

The rose twigs are brightening, hung with
white tufts from deer who dare too close to them.

I am grievous with complaint. I am faithless and sore. It is as if my own hands fell away.

Not May, its musk and bloom. The orchard clings
to burgundy, a russet waste. The packed
soil underneath where cattle, deer sought shade,
is now a rude, abandoned hut that brings
no rest. Misplaced and cool, this fold of earth.
Misplaced the gestures hands will make, collecting
water. The summer flowers are extreme,
a scorch of white. This draught of limbs, this berth
of thorns where I steer clear of you and your
mock chastity. But, look, the birds remain,
off-key, all action. Why? The herbals say
the blue-black haws, their pulp a smear, are for
conditions of the heart, the tortured stem
a sacrament. And I should swallow them.

MOSS

Under each lip,
    in a cranny, a crawl,
the mosses grow overt, triumphant.
There is nothing to hide,
    white bristle, beard,
the intimacy with which they regard
water. Claw-shaped between rains,
    they rain upward,
overcoming the stumps, the ruin
    of heartwood.
Burnt umber: softening of the dead.
Soft beasts, they feed on excrement,
    sopping up the clear
eruption of the springs. With open
mouths, they drink from the cracked
    vault of winter.
Claiming it, they claim absolution.
    Dark sludge, this jasper
that doesn't stain the skin, the release
of the tiny gray moths.
    Parasitic? Yes.
There is a tenderness that comes.
The words we use: to cushion, to cling.

TOBACCO

How can you not want me,
the dark syrup I offer—
or this smoke rising harsh
from the body in l's and s's,
in sketches made with charcoal?
Milton said the angels catch
our desire in their vases, unstopping
the corks for the god to smell.
Brown grains, gilt-edged, the flavor
of cognac—say the word
and I will call them all back to you.
I know I am pernicious, a secret
blown into the ear, something
sacred gotten into the wrong hands.
A pinch, a leaf turned to parchment.
In the beginning was exchange.
There was a lack. I sought to fill it.
So, why now the admonitions?
According to Milton, Eve had
everything she could think to want,
the perfect lover, fruit in season,
a stable home. Then, imagine her
reaching forward, then back.
The feeling must have been exquisite.

BERRIES

In the painting *Gabrielle d'Estrees*
et sa soeur, it is the sister whose nipple
Gabrielle is ready to pluck,
her two fingers, the thumb and the third
pressed around the knot the breast strains
into, pimpled as raspberries, Gabrielle
making the shape of a b for the deaf,
the shape of the hand in the act of meditation,
breathing in and out so that all she can hear
is the clasp and unclasp of her pulse,
and if she brings her hand to her nose,
it is bitter, resinous from the tree this seabird
lands in, and if there is taste,
for one does not pluck without tasting,
it is damp, warm, unsweetened.

ICELANDIC POPPIES

—for Ed

All summer, the poppies held sway in my kitchen garden,
magisterial and tall, a smear of melon.
They were rare birds I tamed, their four tongues
spread wide, each tongue stroked with a brush of violet.
They were so fragile that they would shake in my hands.

My friend came to visit with his black hair dyed yellow.
He was bronze and wrapped in an orange beach towel,
his lover David in dark blue. They were flowers, too,
and I adored their adorations of each other, how
they leaned, kissed poolside as if magnetized by the sun.

Now, one by one, in the shallow rains of late September,
the poppies close. Eventually, they will shatter.
I find their scraps, still fresh, caught on their own gray-green
leaves or brutalized, pressed by rain into the mud.
It is like finding, on the footpath, the body of a tanager

or the bruised peel of nectarine. After the dross of beauty,
what? Seed-heads, frost-blue and shaped like
Byzantine cupolas are rising above the curling, mothy leaves.
The holy kingdom sways in the wind as the petals did.
Its domes are bald and blind, and capped with green stars.

My friends who were in love have gone back
to their separate cities. They say the summer was an illusion,
due to the narcotic of lust. But wait, I call after them,
to have been *drowsed with the fume of poppies!*
To have been rapt! Induced! To have been red chiffon!

CHOKECHERRIES

The Crow call this time of year the Black Cherry Moon
when the rose hips are blood-bright,
spattered on their overwrought stems, and the creek
calls so clearly in words almost our own
as we come sliding down the bank.
Last night, we covered the gardens in plastic.
The chickadees were back after their wide diet of summer.
We ate the last trout, its spine curved from disease.
So much can go wrong, I want to know
what you will promise me as our hands reach in and in
through the copper, the carmine leaves.
I know you are lonely, alone with your grief
for your parents who are not my parents, for your life,
which, despite all, is not my life. The cherries
are thick here, hanging in clusters, purple-black from frost.
It has started to rain and I am chilled by it.
Each day, we promise, we will talk of our fears
of intimacy, how we still expect to be hurt when we love.
You bring me a coat from the back of the truck,
but I want to stop our task now, to sit in the cab
of the truck while the gray spills, slick with thunder.
What if I kissed you there in depth.
After so many years, I can misunderstand the difference
between instinct and obligation, how my hand
continues to grasp the stems. Keats said
poems should come easy as leaves off the trees,

but see how they cling and wrestle with their ties.
And now, the sun shines. It is not this grace
I had imagined. When Keats said poems, I meant
love. The chokecherries roll easily
into my palm, then fall into the plastic bag that binds
my wrist. Over and over, until we have enough,
until our fingers are bruised with their dark juices.

CATTAILS

The listening I do in winter is simple.
I watch you like a stranger. I watch me.
The ditch wheat shudders like tinsel,
a bundled sound. The day-moons appear,
bleached and stiffened. You have hurt me
and I have stayed, believing love to be
endurance, back and forth over the snow crust
until the cattails call to me. Stem, pod,
the color of sheep. In this wind, they shatter.

The cattails are unraveling. Their stuffing
un-stuffs. The tight brown pelts split their seams.
My allegiance is vegetable, here with the stalk.
It is a distaff, un-spinning, the work abandoned.
The seeds are packed too tightly
like a sod-fire without air. No one guesses
the expansion such tightness holds.
My allegiance is ceremonial. I pull things apart,
see how far I can take them past the skin.

I scare myself then, see those things I never say:
that love has failed, that we have chosen safety.
I want to be in danger but with you.
Sweep the seeds out the door, onto the frozen
ground to be tracked in and out by my boots.
Let the drafts in. Let the seeds find their corners.

I give up my strenuous hold. And if
you pull me back, first unwrap my summer clothes.
I will see if it is still possible to fit into them.

ASPEN

Hay-moult. The long summer grasses
stiffen with ice.
Under them, cold water goes spindling.

Delicate is not childlike. The madness
in winter trees, limbs
hoary, kinked from their unbraiding.

Lavender. Dusk. And the aspens climb
the watershed, tower
by white tower, a procession of holy days.

Too much goes by to keep an account of,
chickadees called back
from the tiny flames they tend, the tunnels

mice dig under snow. Thrown like ropes,
they loop across my path.
The snow is thin. They are too visible now.

Out of honor, out of ignorance, I tie green
around a branch—
it looks garish, manufactured, in this light—

because the herbals told me. Because I
saw my life was yellow,
shredded, and must be weighted with quartz

to bring it back. Back is the good road,
those over-spilling days
when my arms divided and twisted into nests.

Speechless, the aspens wait until the leaves
will fill their ears again.
There is the clatter now of owl-wings

in the empty, stunted limbs. The ceremonial
year is over. The give-aways begin.
Is the road so thin and grosgrain between us?

WISTERIA

> Oh, was there not, from the first,
> more poison in thy nature than in mine?
> —*Nathaniel Hawthorne, "Rappaccini's Daughter"*

Here is my father's garden,
the latticework arches.
Here is the mess of his floor.
The camellia petals rain
down and brown
like the white core of apples.
It is my breath,
he says, that fronds them.
I am mist and hysteria,
a whisper through the days.
The thousand tiny smelt
of bay leaves wash ashore.
And I am the ankle-deep
that sweeps them.
Light floods high. The moss
of shadow fingers
surreptitiously through the brick.
For him, I tend the nightshade,
froth of water hemlock.
Only jasmine and wisteria climb.
He swears that I
gave their voices to them,

that we are draped like monkshood,
not shaped like stars.
My intestines glow and wither
as I bend in my father's garden.
One of my breasts
has been removed. Breast, breast,
the clusters hang luxuriant.
Air clots with vanilla and lime.
I thought that once love came,
it would be equal to me,
its fragrance not so faint that I must
force my tongue into its corolla
like the moths who lower
theirs in trains of spit. He tells you
butterflies sink to the stone pavings
when they near her.
He says, the violets you brought her
scorched in her hands.

VIOLETS

In small handfuls,
     like tweezing
         the wings off a moth,
their taste, a tiny blemish on the tongue.
Alyse wants us to take our shoes off
     and hang our feet in the creek.
The largest animal in the world, she says, is god.
The white cat is drugged
     under the porch,
watching the flight and flutter-down of spring.
It is real before we act on it, then it's actual.
Light sways from the south into the yard,
     yellow green each trunk,
                and then we billow.
And what is my image of god,
     a saucer of olive oil,
         a glass of golden wine,
the rose so over-bred it has lost its smell?
I tell her that here in the mountains
     it is important for me to know
that somewhere else there is an ocean.
     And violets?
Shrinking violets because daughter is less than son,
     because daughters
are the frightened ones,
     a covey in the vast green wash-out of the world.

I R I S

---

whatever
returns from oblivion returns
to find a voice
—*Louise Gluck*

The iris bulbs huddle,
their brown rags sopped,
yet above,
the light green flumes
have barely parted.
This is when I love them best
before they speak
and risk it all—
their petals washed out
under the barreling
hooves of the spring.
All night,
the creek moving stones.
I love the birds precisely
because I don't
know what they're singing.
How the iris stay
unblossomed in silt.
What if they recede
like this rain
that rests before it seeps?

How truly imperative is form?
My neighbor believes
that men must learn to be
on earth, and that
women must learn to be gods.
The tiger-striped eye
peeks out from its lids.
Why, it seems to ask,
or why not? I mean,
what does it care
for the future of its tribe?
It lives.
Its life is almost done.
Once a mind was on fire,
then it was quenched with rain,
slowed to ashes and mud.
Better the grace
of one smooth blade repeated,
sealed as a god is sealed,
than to be wrong.

LAUREL

Filled with the voices of the first
and lesser gods—bay laurel, rose hip,
star—I have grown a third sex,
for which I am thrown
like a drunk against the walls.
Shiny and lost, far from the Aegean—
if there is green fallen into the pool,
I will go to it, half-believing,
as if anything could grow in this cold—
cress, or the white flower
of some sprig a deer descending
has scuffed from its hooves. But not so.
The pond is rimmed with
stretch marks of ice. The snow
is a tourniquet over the watering,
and this, only the needles of fir.
Yes, I overreact to every
provocation. I was rude to your god
but he is well past his prime.
If I come to the clearing
and find what you have left for him,
on the stump of a tree you felled,
I will steal it for the waxwings,
the eggs for the ravens, the berries
black, wrinkled like frozen thumbs.

If sin is a prophesy,
it is a leaf between my teeth.
In women, they often call this nerves.

WILLOW

A sibyl, her body wracked by the god's voice
entering, bounces
off the walls of the cave, her mouth splintered.

I am the shape of a woman's madness,
and the exorcism of that madness.
I am a fountain frozen into pewter and stone.

I will tell you what I know. There are no words
for my transgressions, only the space
between the leaving of one god for another,

a male for a female, fraught with fear. But I
have passed it. I am the shape
your fingers draw when they circle for an opening,

a mow of half-dead twigs, fallow and new green.
Hell is what I make of it,
the twisting away from what must be accepted

until my limbs turn muffled, censorious, gray.
You call this decay, but what is it really?
I am the shape of hysteria, a hollowed-out home

for mold, the sea-blue froth of lichen. Sit with me
awhile. You, too, are growing old.
What if the sibyl called the voice of god her own?

By now, we both know that winter will be back.
The white geese will orbit without ruse,
and still, these new shoots, like snakes rising

on end, like bronze flames there to consume me.
Is it me? The sound of the water
is rarefied, near. The bright irritation of buds.

BALSAM

Go, with all your dead, crying
for the broken, crow-voiced,
rigorous, the clatter-trap
of the young. May you bargain
clandestinely, provoke a wide
chastity, eat maple cakes,
or ride ox-carts if you want.
You can't use me for your prayers.
I will sit here, on my thatch
of sweet needles, inside
the unglazed curve of my arms.
Here, with all I've gathered,
the pink and the bisque,
from the dark criss-crossing
of my childhood among forests.
For there are no corners
in this suffering. I grow my hair
with its soot and its tangles,
but I start out in earnestness.
Yes, I dismantled the charm.
I took the turquoise ring and dangled
it from my ear before I lost it.
The white rocks from the dream
I scattered. For years, only mud,
the oily black feathers on the trail.
Convince me there is happiness.

Not you. Not you. The gods line up
with their badly built temples,
one father after another. Shadows
between trunks on the ridge.
What a relief it used to be, to feel
their gold eyes on me.

Green slash of the world. Water
in shade, the smell of stewing
lemons. I promise:
I will begin again, not with false joy
but with the smoke
of my breath after the kiss,
the one where I am left alone again.

JUNIPER

Supplicant, low-lying, as if their arms
hugged the knees of some host,
their backs, the piss-green tatter of winds—

Who will recognize them? The wooden spears
of their spines stiffen with sap,
atrophy. They are evergreen, slow-ripening,

yielding only a few berries at a time: hard,
dark, the nipples of some god we
dare not pluck. Not pure. Pure is undivided.

What part don't they show the sun? The blue
blaze on their palms they hide
from the sky, some strange kind of reversal.

Astringent, adversarial. They persist in the evil
of grappling. Rejection and praise.
The small retractions I have learned to call sin.

Daphne, the ancients say, turned into a bay tree
to escape the rape of Apollo.
And Leda? Old school. To be taken unaware.

But to fall back as if expecting someone there
to catch you, to be a raft in a great river?
It's not I who calls this blasphemous. Just that lust

in a woman is so very unexpected. Bitter-fresh,
intoxicant, the berries blue with age.
They are trying to make incense of themselves.

FERN

Seep and hollow, we have entered the fold
where the smoke from our fires draws the low clouds to it,
where the waters pick and pick at the black roots of alder,
the tea-dark into which the springs slide.

They slide over the crab-legged stems of winter willow,
between snowberries—corn-shaped—the blackbirds
fish the air for, the blossom of coyote track
pressed into snow, and these fine finger-bones of bracken.

The frozen earth denies. Everywhere, signs of molting.
Mulch-light, the maiden hair is choking the rivulets.
Its henna, its curls. This could be the site
of a hundred shorn women, or the rites of their slaying.

We are told that it was beautiful when Ophelia
was drowning, her hair lavish as a fever over the cool beds.
She rose and sunk under the weight
of the alluvial, the urge for another life that pressed upon her.

To surrender is not grace, but to move without impediment?
The earth here is cold, and reluctant.
Nowhere else in the world did the world match her singing
or her stress. Ice-fronds. Foliage. The ferns into currents.

Though she, too, died for love, Ophelia did not resurrect
from the red-haired disaster of her winter sleeping.

So, we live in a fiction of limits,
not possibilities, and think we do not have a god behind us.

Here, like a god in its particular uncurling, a bracken fan—brilliant—
dips its fin into the stream.
There is the loud lap and snort of an animal trapped under ice.
There is a woman's veil shrunk to a religion of brown.

Through snow-pock up, through sludge,
through basket-dim the loom-slits shining,
a patch of rush under the fir.
The alder skin stretched tight, polished.
Up through bronze root,
contraction, the cacophony of melt.
All soul, in the basin
near the lap and shore of ice. The oldest
anchorite. Up through the buried
before there was a time, the knowing
from the inside out.
Hollow and stemmed, sterile, alive—
the tender brown spores come first.
Before female, male,
they collide in new heat. Breakers,
barely shoot, they are moored.
Not gods, which we might blaspheme,
they are close-hatched, cerebral.
Every time they close their eyes,
they go to sleep. Onions
make them drowsy and winter is
the largest one, layer on layer,
earth wrapped in its yellow skin.
All the dead are yellow then, yarrow
and mullein. Ice cracks, when it cracks,
snaking fast across its shield.

They lie on the floor, sour from waiting.
Our dear near-fish, for it is
from here they have climbed back,
slipping off the bank into deep again.

NIGHTSHADE

In the small hours, here is something I can eat
with which I am familiar, perfume
of wood and fruit, the elasticity of plums.
Each berry is crimson and tainted as blood.
What else could I pack to take with me?
The year is closing. The slumped marsh grasses
are yellow with the twilight the hunters
seem to love, when the animals must stand still
to be saved. Chill is the falling through
the flood-dam of the bank. Chill is the sun
as I stare and it stares, so weakened that we don't
turn away. There is bear scat everywhere,
the huge brown logs seeded with pits—
but I am weaning myself of the world's excess.
My lips split in the night and stain the white sheets.
I am being called to the religious order
of the leaves. What should I wear? I rub the dirt
from my clothes, my papery clothes turning gray.
These exits are always frantic, though habitual.
There's always a mistake and I am the one
who makes it. I look back. The fruit is red. I eat.
Later, I must account for the clots on the trail.
I must call the changes winds,
and hide my hands which smell of vineyards.
Twice now, I have seen the nightshade
growing in the wastes, or by the farm yard gate,

and plucked it. It is hard not to think
there will be other women in Hades, pushed
like seeds into the darkness
until the darkness softens into what is light.
Because we will fail that, too.
Stripped of the berries, the wooden stems rise
in tier after tier, their star-seats wooden,
and vanquished. And our flesh
will brighten the thrones we are ripped from.

SALSIFY

...born in the infinite disorder of prayers
                                                —*André Breton*

We are the undisciplined, of smaller mind,
white sun multiplied and gone to seed.
Wind, raise us
like china plates from the suds.
Raise us with your promise of rinsing.
The tiny purple grains trail
from shocks of timothy. Breast-feathers
are plucked from the thistle.
And our strange globes, each
isolate, appear,
not all at once like dandelions in the field.
The trees are perfect. They remember
their color, the correct order of its will.
Black birch turns butter and lingers,
the alder blackens and curls.
Then one cloud tears itself from the southeast
and here, the others follow.
In sleep, small birds tighten their claws
and drift, leaving their bodies to this world.
The fish dreams, a steadying
out of the current. No one talks of control.
Once, we were yellow, emblematic,
marked by the bright slivers of our bloom.

To get from that to this, we must be
unafraid of the small expansions of emptiness.
We must billow, knot, and take the rack.
We, who are a collection
of old sayings, all have the same message:
Detach. Detach, feel the tug
at your scalp. A yard light glows from the top
of its stalk and finds its way
into the darkest crooks of the field.
What do we know of the imminent good?
We have feathers
and the rough-scaled anchor of seeds.
Seeds? Not now. Bless this time
when we desist, apostate and distracted,
eluding the rough edges of our end.

PRAIRIE SAGE

She began her own litany of berries . . .
                                    —*Derek Walcott*

White-beaded, the raceme
and the pale blue buntings of the leaves—
blue and I am smeared with it,
dried in north light.
It is a ghost-bundle, bleached
as the light is— not entirely. There is often
shade to hide in, the oblong cast
beyond the canyon where the ferns grow.
The snow-seams are blue,
and the under-wings of the swan,
the spring sky so dull that color vanishes.
Invisible, the chime of waxwings.
How can I compare?
When I do, I am found wanting, inglorious.
Claw-footed and torn like the bird
from its limb, the roots are
featherless, tissue-wrapped, archival.
What bride would carry this,
so delicate in its drying, in its almost-color,
from which I tear scraps,
small as sentences. Crisp and crumbled,
the sharp inland smell is a menthol

used for purification. For years
I have picked at it, its upside-down haze.
A woman's impotence is not
what we speak of.
But here it is, dogged, invested with swirl.
To burn. To make myself worthy.
Not worthy yet to the wildly unprecedented,
the flight of starlings or these stars,
clustered on an ashen stem. Listen,
the trees are making a soft row by the river.
They were deranged by the winter.
See the mess they've made of growth.
A bouquet? A bride's bouquet
of sage and all she knows. Subjugated,
so we can search for her. Doubted, so we can
dream of her. As lackluster. Frenzied.
The blue lobes curled in. What then?

Rinse as water rinses through the stones.
Add dry straw to the putrid.
The pale blue necks collapse in the heat.
Their smoke will be my smoke.

MELISSA KWASNY is the author of a book of poetry, *The Archival Birds* (Bear Star Press, 2000), and editor of *Toward the Open Field: Poets on the Art of Poetry 1800 - 1950* (Wesleyan University Press, 2004). She has also published two novels, most recently, *Trees Call for What They Need*. Ms. Kwasny lives in Jefferson City, Montana.